Published by Creative Education
P.O. Box 227, Mankato, Minnesota 56002
Creative Education is an imprint of
The Creative Company
www.thecreativecompany.us

Design by The Design Lab
Production by Chelsey Luther
Art direction by Rita Marshall
Printed in the United States of America

Photographs by Dreamstime (Mandimiles,
Outdoorsman, Joanne Weston), Getty Images (Flip
Nicklin), iStockphoto (Jo Ann Crebbin, Dale Walsh),
Shutterstock (CampCrazy Photography, Phillip Dyhr
Hobbs, TsuneoMP), SuperStock (NHPA, Minden
Pictures, Pacific Stock-Design Pics, Stock Connection)

Library of Congress Cataloging-in-Publication Data
Riggs, Kate.
Whales / Kate Riggs.
p. cm. — (Amazing animals)
Summary: A basic exploration of the appearance,
behavior, and habitat of whales, the large ocean animals. Also included is a story from folklore explaining
why New Zealanders traditionally rode whales.
Includes bibliographical references and index.
ISBN 978-1-60818-351-7
1. Whales—Juvenile literature. I. Title.

QL737.C4R54 2014
599.5—dc23   2013005400

First Edition
9 8 7 6 5 4 3 2 1

AMAZING ANIMALS
WHALES

BY KATE RIGGS

CREATIVE EDUCATION

Humpback whales
are baleen whales
that live in all oceans

A whale is an **ocean** animal. There are 25 kinds of whales that have teeth. Thirteen kinds of whales do not have teeth. These whales are called baleen whales.

ocean   a big area of deep, salty water

*Minke whales
(opposite) are darker
than belugas (left)*

Whales have long bodies that are good for swimming. Their skin is smooth. Most whales are a dark color such as brown or gray. Beluga whales are all white.

Whales are some of the biggest animals in the world. Small whales are nine feet (2.7 m) long. The blue whale is the largest whale. It can be as long as 100 feet (30 m). The biggest blue whales can weigh 200 tons (181 t)!

A blue whale's heart weighs as much as a car

Whales are found in all of Earth's oceans. They swim by moving their tail and flippers. A whale's tail has two flat pads at the end. These pads are called flukes. Blue whales can swim 20 miles (32 km) per hour!

A whale may raise its flukes in the air when it dives

*Baleen is made of
the same material as
human fingernails*

Baleen whales eat small ocean animals, fish, and **plankton**. The baleen in a baleen whale's mouth looks like a comb. It traps tiny creatures in the whale's mouth. Toothed whales feed on larger **prey**. They might like to eat fish, squid, and even seals.

plankton tiny water creatures

prey animals that are killed and eaten by other animals

A humpback calf swims close by its mother

A mother whale has one **calf** at a time. The calf is born in the water. It has to swim to the surface to breathe air. Whales breathe through one or two blowholes on their head. Calves drink their mother's milk. They stay with their mothers for up to a year.

calf a baby whale

Some whales live in groups called pods. Baleen whales make singing sounds to talk to each other. Toothed whales click, whistle, squeak, and groan. Most whales live for 40 to 85 years in the wild.

Sometimes humpbacks group together to find food

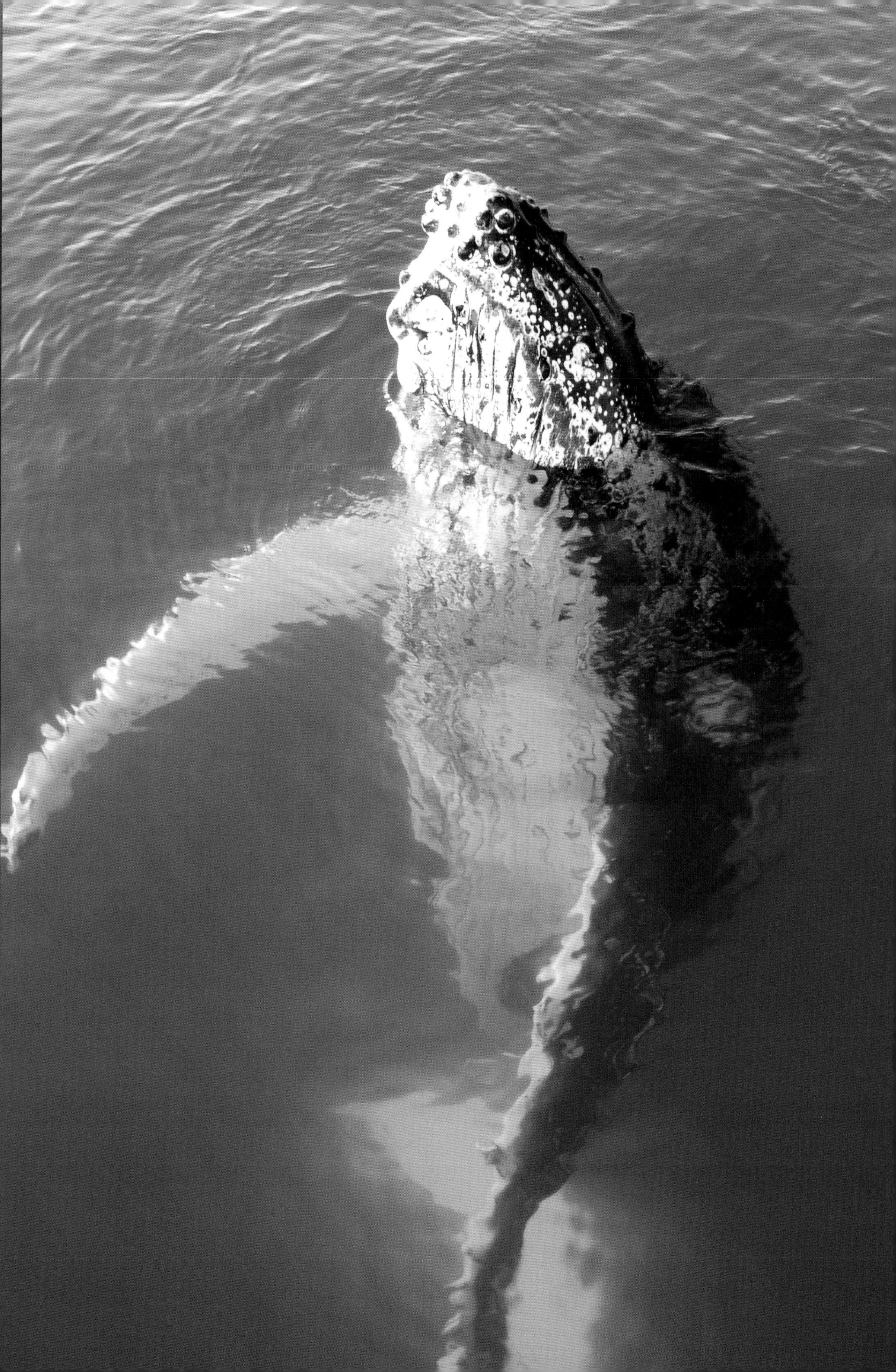

Whales hunt for food.

They talk to each other. They jump out of the water and splash back down. Sometimes whales poke their heads out of the water. This is called spy-hopping.

Spy-hopping whales can stay upright for several minutes

When whales leap out of the water, it is called breaching

People go on special boats to watch whales. Sometimes whales can be seen in big groups. They may be feeding or **migrating**. It is fun to watch these big animals swim and dive!

migrating moving from place to place during different parts of the year

A *Whale Story*

Why did people in New Zealand ride whales long ago? The Maori people of New Zealand tell a story about a man named Paikea. Paikea was almost drowned at sea when his boat sank. But a humpback whale saved him. The whale took Paikea to New Zealand. Then Paikea became a great leader. Later, Maori people rode whales to show they could be strong leaders.